A LETTER TO MY BROTHERS

MEMORIES
OF REGRET

CHRISHANA GREER

Paperback ISBN: 978-1-955411-42-4
E-book ISBN: 978-1-955411-37-0
Hardcover ISBN: 978-1-955411-38-7

Printed by Davis and Greer Publishing
in the United States of America

CONTENTS

CHAPTER 1

A Letter.. 5

CHAPTER 2

Marcus... 7

CHAPTER 3

Vonte.. 21

CHAPTER 4

Memories of Regret... 35

CHAPTER 5

Message to My Brothers 41

CHAPTER 1
A Letter

I never truly realized how much I needed both of you until I no longer had you. Maybe that was my own naiveness, thinking you would never leave. How could I fathom the thought of you being gone when you had always given me reasons to believe you would be near?

CHAPTER 2
Marcus

Marcus, you were the first one to
leave me. I was only fifteen.

The stories surrounding your death taught me early that friends are not always what they claim to be. I picture you lying in the hallway, gasping for air, using your last breath to call for your best friend. Instead of staying with you, he left.

He didn't run for help. He didn't call family.
He didn't even dial 911. He just left you.

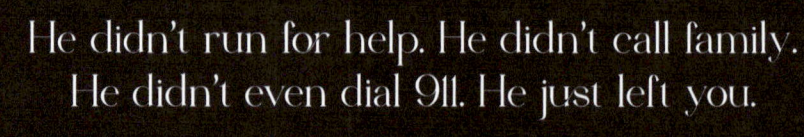

How could someone you knew your whole life, someone you trusted enough to call your brother, leave you to die? Maybe you loved him more than he loved you.

That betrayal hurt. But not as much
as my own last words to you.

I remember sitting on the small couch in your room while you sat up on the edge of your twin-sized bed. You teased me, saying, *"Michelle said I can whoop you."* Only fifteen, but thinking I was grown, I shot back with remarks I'd rather not repeat, too ashamed to admit those might have been my final words.

My final interaction with you. While never realizing how childish I sounded. We started play-fighting. I scratched you by accident and when I saw blood, I panicked.

I ran to the bathroom, grabbed a wet tissue,
and patted your neck, whispering, *"I'm sorry."*
You didn't get mad. You just looked at
me out the corner of your eye, quiet,
letting me tend to the tiny wound.

I didn't know those would be
our last moments together.

When the phone call came that you had been shot, I thought, *He'll be okay. He'll come home and joke, "I'm Lil Dude, not even a gunshot wound could kill me."* I never imagined I had already seen you for the last time.

I am sorry. Sorry that my last words were a smart remark. Sorry for not saying, "I love you." Sorry for taking time with you for granted.

Losing you taught me something I will never forget: Be mindful of the words you speak. You never know which ones will be the last.

CHAPTER 3
Vonte

Then it was you, Vonte.

Your death forced me to realize that life is bigger than what's happening in my own world. I couldn't imagine you leaving, yet suddenly there I was, standing at your hospital bed.

A tube was down your throat. Machines breathed for you. I begged you to move, just once. A tear, a finger twitch, anything to show you were still fighting. I stared at the monitor, hoping it would climb past two heartbeats, showing you were breathing on your own.

I didn't want to believe you were leaving me.
But I also couldn't convince myself you
would be okay. Not this time.

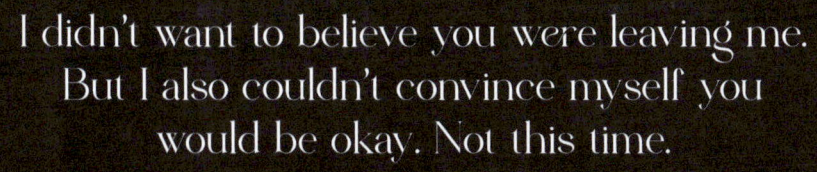

I went to the only place that ever made me feel safe, Marcus's grave. I stood there begging him to watch over you, to protect you the way he always protected me. But I couldn't feel him near me. And not long after, I got the call. You were gone.

The anger boiled.
At Marcus for not protecting you.
At life for taking you.
At everything.

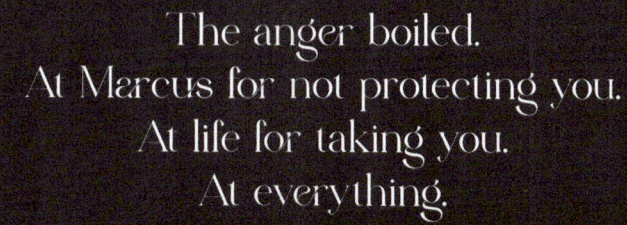

You were stabbed, for no reason, by people I will never understand, in the middle of the night. You were hurting inside, I knew that. Maybe that's why you walked for hours, zoned out, unaware of danger around you.

I believed you would overcome it, like you always had. I dreamed we would go to counseling together one day, open up about what we bottled inside, finally heal together. But that chance never came.

After you died, I scrolled through our messages and stared at the three pictures I had of you. That's when I realized, all you really wanted was time with me.

The constant texts, asking me to come over, asking what I was doing, asking me to drive you somewhere. Those weren't about the errands. You just wanted to be around me.

But I was caught up in my own world.
My dry replies, "Nothing," or
"I'm not coming out," feel like a knife now.
I said no when I could have said yes.

Now all I have are the memories we did make
and the imaginary ones we never got to.

CHAPTER 4
Memories of Regret

I never realized how little time I had with either of you, only because I never expected to live without you.

Life is unpredictable. When death comes, it forces us to face our faults, the times we didn't say, "*I love you*," the moments we wasted.

Losing you both came like a storm
I didn't see coming, leaving me with
two things: the memories we did share,
which I will always cherish, and the
regrets of the ones we never created.

As I grow without you physically here,
I will carry both. And I will let those regrets
teach me to cherish the people I still have,
to embrace them fully while they are alive.

The hardest thing about having siblings is when you are forced to say goodbye. A goodbye you never thought would come so soon. A goodbye that makes uncertainty permanent. It forces you to prepare for unspoken goodbyes, carrying only the memories and the what-ifs forever.

CHAPTER 5
Message to My Brothers

Writing this book has been my way
to pour out pain and regret, to say the
things I never got to say.

I apologize for not valuing our time the way
I should have. For not creating more
everlasting memories.

I never imagined life without you, yet here I am, carrying both love and regret. But your loss has taught me something priceless: to hold tight to the people I love while they are still here.

Your lives may have ended, but your presence stays with me. In memory, in spirit, in every lesson you left behind.

Always,
Your sister

46

www.ingramcontent.com/pod-product-compliance
Lightning Source LLC
Chambersburg PA
CBHW040849120626
46547CB00001B/89